DOGS

GALLERY BOOKS

An Imprint of W. H. Smith Publishers Inc.
112 Madison Avenue
New York City 10016

This edition first published in U.S.
in 1990 by Gallery Books,
an imprint of W.H. Smith Publishers, Inc.
112 Madison Avenue, New York, New York 10016

ISBN 0-8317-9575-1

Printed and bound in Spain

For rights information about the photographs in
this book please contact:

The Image Bank
111 Fifth Avenue, New York, NY 10003

Producer: Solomon M. Skolnick
Author: Jill Caravan
Design Concept: Lesley Ehlers
Designer: Ann-Louise Lipman
Editor: Sara Colacurto
Production: Valerie Zars
Photo Researcher: Edward Douglas
Assistant Photo Researcher: Robert V. Hale
Editorial Assistant: Carol Raguso

Title page: Whether purebred or of mixed breed, most dogs have the intelligence to learn a variety of basic commands and comply with the family's daily routine. *Opposite:* This profile of a collie shows this gentle breed's trademark semi-erect ears and long snout.

Anyone who has ever had the pleasure of owning a dog knows the rewards that come with these special relationships. Obedience and loyalty are two of the characteristics traditionally associated with the domestic dog, and dog owners everywhere can attest to the existence of these and other qualities which they feel truly make the dog "man's best friend."

The dog is, in fact, one of two families of animals (the other is the cat family) that has been, throughout history, befriended by humankind, taken into both our homes and our hearts.

The domestic dog, *Canis familiaris* is one of the 38 species of the dog family, *Canidae* which also includes the wolf, the fox, and the coyote. It is generally considered the first domestic animal, having existed with man as a companion and household pet since the days of the cave dwellers.

It is believed that the direct ancestor of the dog is the wolf, originally found in Europe, Asia, and North America. This animal was actually the first dog to be domesticated. Early man offered food and protection to the wild ancestor of today's dog, in exchange for its performance of certain hunting-related duties. Cave dwellers used the dog for its keen hunting instincts and for protection.

Top to bottom: **The rough-coated collie is, by far, the most popular of all varieties of collie. Long ago, the collie existed as a herding dog in Scotland and England, and probably got its name from the black-faced, black-footed Colley sheep that it guarded. They are gentle, loyal, and obedient, a devoted family dog in almost any situation.**

One of Britain's oldest breeds, the bearded collie is valued as a shepherd and drover, always ready for service with a bright, curious expression. *Below:* Intelligent, sensitive, and easy to train, the collie's long, dense hair requires careful daily brushing.

Later civilizations used dogs as guards, companions, and message carriers in times of war.

As the dog took a more active role in the daily lives of humans, it became the object of many myths and supernatural stories.

There are legends, mainly in Europe, of dogs who have returned from the grave as ghost-dogs to guard their loved ones. Some of these dogs are attached to families – others have appeared on roads or in churches. They have been described as black or white, sometimes ghost-like, sometimes solid in form.

One bizarre tale tells of poodles that jumped on people's shoulders, forcing them to the ground. These phantoms were said to be demons or the Devil himself. Christian symbols like the crucifix and the rosary were used to ward off these demon-dogs.

Dogs have also reportedly taken the form of witch familiars, or evil spirits embodied in animals. Unlike the infamous cat familiars, which are closely associated with witches, the dog familiar appears only on occasion, usually during crises.

The lore of the dog goes back to ancient mythology. Many of the companions of Celtic gods and heroes were magical dogs. The sun god, Lugh, had a magic hound which turned into a ball of fire every night.

In Hindu mythology, Yama, god of the dead, who had two insatiable dogs, each with four eyes and expanded nostrils, often assumed canine form.

In Greek mythology, Cerberus, the hound of Hell, had up to 50 heads and was chained to the gates of Hades, where he devoured any living being who tried to cross the threshold of the Underworld.

There are many legends of dogs whose fidelity continued after the death of their owners, and of those that died out of love for their masters. In Homer's "Odyssey," Ulysses returned home after twenty years to be greeted by his dog, Argus. Recognizing his master, Argus wagged his tail with joy, dropped his ears – and died.

The Shetland sheepdog hails from the Shetland Islands, where only the hardiest can survive. A collie in miniature, the breed stands between 13 and 16 inches high at the shoulder. *Below:* For its work as a leader of the blind, the German shepherd must exhibit a high order of intelligence and discrimination. Patience, observation, faithfulness, and good judgment are just a few of its outstanding qualities. *Opposite:* The quintessential work dog, the German shepherd has been used as a police dog, rescue dog, war dog, and herder.

Preceding page: Although its name implies Australian origin, the Australian shepherd was developed in the United States. *This page, top:* This pure white Samoyed, amid a bed of flowers, is out of its tundra element. Samoyeds are good-natured and affectionate, and love to play with children. *Below:* Often mistaken for a fluffy, white teddy bear, the young Samoyed has an icy white coat that must be cared for with daily brushing and periodic baths.

Other tales tell of dogs who jumped onto funeral pyres and were burned to death with their masters. In some cultures, dogs were killed and buried with their masters to guide them through the Underworld. Deceased dogs were fitted with glass eyes so they could see in the afterlife.

The loyalty went both ways. Egyptian masters mourned the loss of their dogs by shaving their heads and bodies. They erected tombs for them and fitted them with golden masks.

In China, thousands of years ago, the Pekingese were revered as Imperial dogs, and were treated as divine in life and death. In Tibet, dogs were bred in monasteries and trained by monks to take part in religious rituals.

In Greek and Roman cults, dogs were kept in temples where they participated in the religious rites of the gods. Sacred dogs have also been bred with white blazes on their foreheads, in imitation of Buddah.

A creation myth tells of God placing a dog on guard in paradise, and Bible lore credits dogs for using their noses to plug the holes in Noah's ark, the reason for the dog's cold nose.

Popular as a sled dog, the Siberian husky is a naturally friendly and gentle companion, free from the strong odor that many dense-coated breeds carry. *Opposite:* The posture of this Siberian husky shows the strength and stamina that allowed the breed to serve as a search and rescue unit in Byrd's Antarctic expeditions and during wars.

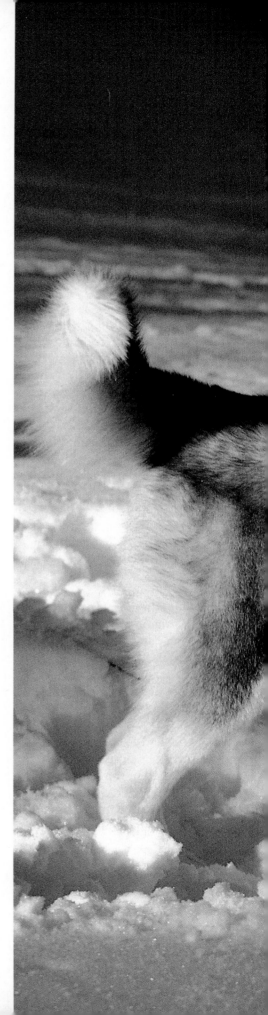

The body of the Alaskan Malamute is slightly longer than it is tall, moving its center of gravity back, allowing for a powerful leaning stance. *Below:* The Alaskan Malamute, a popular breed in cold climates, is capable of pulling one-ton loads over short distances and is sometimes entered in weight-pulling contests. *Opposite:* Often confused with the Siberian husky, the Alaskan Malamute was named after the native Innuit Mahlemuts, who settled along the shores of Kotzebue Sound, Alaska.

One of four varieties of Swiss mountain dog and a cousin to the St. Bernard, the Bernese mountain dog is found mainly on farms in the midland of Switzerland. *Opposite:* The St. Bernard is named after the Great St. Bernard Pass in the Swiss Alps, where they were used to rescue travelers overcome by the elements. Fortunately, this breed likes cold weather.

A Spanish Nativity legend says that the Three Wise Men were each accompanied by a dog to the manger. Any dog named after these companions – Cubillon, Melampo, and Lubino – is said to be blessed.

Some people claim that they and others are descended from dogs, and some saints, including St. Christopher of the Eastern Orthodox Church, are represented as dogs.

Many cultures thought the dog played a role in healing. In China it was believed that disease came from the earth and a dog could be used as a weight to keep it in.

Because of its short legs and long body, climbing stairs can be a harmful activity for the fox-like Welsh corgi. *Left:* There are two types of Welsh corgi, the Cardigan and the Pembroke. England's Queen Elizabeth has been known to raise the latter of this small shepherd breed.

Keeshond, the national dog of Holland, has long served on the barges of the Rhine River. It is known as a good watchdog. *Below:* The Rottweiler, adept at intimidating other dogs and people, carried food for Roman soldiers as they crossed Europe.

Many dogs have been sacrificed and their blood used to ward off evil spirits. The dog has also been ritually eaten in the belief that its good qualities would be acquired, and various parts of the dog were used for medicinal purposes.

In many places, the dog was believed to be able to predict the future, especially death, by howling, and the weather, by movements or actions. Even today, when the moon is full, some dogs let out a very unsettling wolf-like howl.

Like other members of the dog family, *C. familiaris* exhibits great genetic variability. Natural selection and selective breeding have resulted in the development of more than 300 breeds throughout the world. These breeds differ sharply in appearance, function, and size. Weights can vary from one and one-half pounds up to 200 pounds, and heights, which are usually measured from the shoulder, range from six to 36 inches.

Generally, a one-year-old dog can be considered a sexually mature adult. Female dogs go into heat, or become sexually active, approximately every six months. Males will respond accordingly to this cycle. Gestation time in all breeds is approximately nine weeks.

Litter sizes vary depending on the size and weight of the breed. Toy dogs, characteristically tiny, usually produce no more than two puppies; larger breeds may have litters of up to ten. Most mothers are very attentive, cleansing and nursing their newborns.

As a puppy grows, it goes through stages not unlike a human being: childhood, teenage, adulthood, and old age. A pet of two compares to a human in its mid-twenties. After age two, each dog year equals approximately five human years. The lifespan of a dog can be as short as ten years, as with the boxer, or as long as 16 years, in the case of some Lhasa Apsos.

Breeds have been conveniently classified into groups; such classifications, and the breeds within them, vary slightly from country to country. In the United States, the American Kennel Club (AKC) officially recognizes more than 130 breeds in seven different groups. They are: the sporting group, the hound group, the working group, the terrier group, the toy group, the non-sporting group, and the herding group, which until recently was part of the working group.

Standards of desired sizes, colors, and conformation for each breed are established by committees elected by members of various kennel clubs specializing in each breed. In the United States, these standards must be approved by the AKC. Issued since 1929, today's breeding standards represent an ideal dog and are used as guides for breeders and dog show judges in evaluating the quality of each dog. Using these standards and keeping in mind the dog's unique sensory, communicative, and pack characteristics, breeders have been able to develop breeds with the best of these traits.

The name of the Great Dane is a translation of an old French designation, "grand Danois," meaning "big Danish." This breed actually hails from Germany, not Denmark.

Cousin to practically all recognized breeds of the bulldog, the boxer was used in dogfighting and bullbaiting until the popularity of those sports declined. *Left:* Often used as a police dog, watchdog, and guide dog, the boxer is a good-natured and loyal animal. Unfortunately, it usually lives no longer than ten years. *Opposite:* Used as a watchdog and bodyguard, the Doberman pinscher can be aggressive at times.

Other classifying organizations throughout the world include the United Kennel Club (UKC), The Kennel Club of Great Britain (TKC), the Canadian Kennel Club (CKC) and the Federation Cynologique Internationale (FCI) world registry.

Dogs are a marvel of design and instinct. The cold nose of the family dog, for example, is more than just a source of rude, early morning awakenings. Aside from its biological use as a way to regulate temperature, it provides a powerful sense of smell – approximately 500 times stronger than that of humans – and helps dogs to orient themselves to their environment.

The bulldog has an extremely short face, with a short, broad muzzle and a deep fold from the corner of its eye to the corner of its mouth. *Below:* The bulldog was named after the sport of bullbaiting, in which bulls were chased by dogs. *Opposite:* Known for its widespread shoulders and rolling gait, the bulldog shares a common ancestor with the mastiff. Because of its build, it is difficult to mate and whelp.

The loose skin of the China-bred Shar Pei's "horse coat" enabled it to turn on an opponent in a dog fight, even when held firmly in the opposing dog's jaw. Now bred mainly as a companion dog, it is tranquil and loving. *Opposite:* The exaggerated skin folds of the Shar Pei are a deliberate mutation that leads people to refer to it as "the wrinkled dog."

These standard poodle puppies are likely to reach 15 inches in height at the shoulder and mature into gentle companions, suitable for any home. *Opposite:* The short curling coats of these miniature poodles have been cut in what the American Kennel Club calls the "sporting clip." Descended from a French waterdog called the barbet, the poodle was once known for its ability to hunt truffles and retrieve game from marshes.

Dogs also have good eyesight, specially adapted to a daily cycle that favors dawn and dusk. They have an advantage over humans in that their eyes have a light-reflecting layer at the back, which acts as an intensifying device and enables them to make optimum use of existing light. It is this reflection that seems to make their eyes glow in the dark.

Dogs have a very wide field of vision – 250 degrees – as compared to the human's 180. Additionally, their eyes are more sensitive to movement than to detail. That is, they see movement rather than color. Although they see mostly black and white, they are able to distinguish some color, mostly pastels.

Hearing is another highly developed sense. With low-pitched sounds, the dog's ears have about the same ability as humans. Their ability to pick up ultrasonic vibrations, however, allows them to hear sounds that cannot be heard by the average person. Dogs often use this sense to detect when a family member is about to return to the house – amazingly, they are able to discriminate between the sounds of different cars from incredible distances.

The dog's mouth is just as important as its nose, with a well-developed sense of taste closely linked to its sense of smell. The tongue is used for lapping water, eating food, cleaning the body, licking wounds, feeling objects, and expressing affection.

The canine's 42 teeth, whose position and bite vary from breed to breed, are often evident when a dog pants. Since dogs do not perspire, they must pant to cool the body down after exercise or during periods of hot weather.

Two members of the chow chow breed lived with President Calvin Coolidge at the White House. A stamp of the breed is the black-pigmented lips, gums, and tongue. *Below:* **The name chow chow comes from the pidgin-English term "chow chow," which described novelties, curios, and dogs from the Orient.** *Opposite:* **Dalmations are clean and alert with a great passion for hunting. Sometimes, the blue-eyed puppies and their littermates have hearing defects or are totally deaf.**

All of these sensory sources, plus the tail and general body positions, are used by the dog to communicate. The sounds that emanate from a dog's mouth include barking, to threaten, get attention, or express excitement; groaning, to express relief or exhaustion; growling, as a threat or a warning; howling, to convey severe distress or loneliness (wild dogs howl to call other members of the pack); whining, to get attention or for distress; and yelping, usually when in pain.

Besides hearing, the ears are used for expression. They are often pushed up, down, forward, and backward to convey anything from interest to fear and aggression.

As commonly thought, a wagging tail is not necessarily a sign of friendliness, but is actually a sign of conflict in a dog's mind. It really wants to advance, perhaps because of food, companionship, or aggression, but it also wants to retreat because of fear. A wagging tail may symbolize all of these unresolved emotions.

A hanging tail is usually a sign of submission, but this and all other tail positions must be read as signs in conjunction with other expressions, postures, and actions. These signals vary greatly from dog to dog and from breed to breed.

Top to bottom: **The Australian terrier is one of the smallest working terriers — about 10 inches high at the shoulder and only up to 14 pounds in weight. Puppies should be housebroken as early as possible. Excessive body length is a trait of the Skye terrier, which has very short legs and both prick and drop ears.**

Mascot of the students at Cambridge University, the Norwich terrier is believed to be descended from the Trumpington terrier. *Below:* Sometimes called "America's national dog," the Boston terrier is an intelligent, lovable companion. Despite selective breeding, it can still be somewhat aggressive, so it makes a terrific guard dog.

The smooth fox is an especially energetic dog, whose ancestry dates back to ancient times. *Opposite:* At one time, the bullterrier was a ferocious fighting dog. Modern day breeding has made it considerably gentle, as well as loyal, polite, and obedient. The breed enjoys affection although it can be aggressive now and then.

Of the dog's basic instincts (like the need for food, water, mating, territorial marking, and aggressiveness toward or fear of other animals), the pack instinct is one that affects just about everything it does.

In canine society, there is a class system consisting of top dogs, middle dogs, and bottom dogs. When introduced to the human household, the pet dog instinctively sees its human family as the dominant member of the group, or pack, and, therefore, the top dog; hence its tendency toward obedience and loyalty. Its ability to know that it is part of a group, as well as its place in the established hierarchy, drives a dog throughout its life and enables humans to train and use it in various ways.

When a dog is classified as a particular type of dog, such as a working or a sporting dog, it is often associated with the duties or feats that those types are known for. The truth is, most dogs can learn anything if adequately trained. The average dog is as intelligent as a human four-year-old, and despite the myth that "you can't teach an old dog new tricks," a dog can be taught new "tricks" or "jobs" throughout its life.

Herding is perhaps what dogs are best known for. Herding dogs, such as the German shepherd and the Shetland sheepdog, combine what is called an "eye," an intense unblinking gaze to control livestock, with other tactics like heel nipping and corralling, by running back and forth.

Top to bottom: **The abundant, hanging fur of the squat Pekingese drags along the ground, bringing a good amount of dirt into the house. Originally from Mexico, the Chihuahua is the smallest breed in the world, weighing in at under 6 pounds. The papillion, one of two breeds of continental toy spaniel, needs careful grooming.**

Historically dogs have been used for hunting. Those breeds that have a keen sense of smell, such as hounds, pointers, retrievers, and terriers, are usually employed for this work. These dogs are skillful at sniffing out and flushing prey, and eventually fetching it for their human hunting companions.

Some dogs, whose fur has adapted to sub-freezing temperatures and whose muscles have proven amazingly strong, are used in the Arctic as sled dogs, for search and rescue, and for sport. Other dogs, such as the greyhound and the whippet of the hound group, have long legs and lean bodies which make them ideal for racing.

Dogs like the German shepherd have long been used in police work. Trained to use their sense of smell to sniff out fugitives, drugs, and other illegal substances, they are often used to detect contraband brought into international airports. These dogs are well respected members of law-enforcement teams and have been known to receive rewards and pensions for their work.

In ancient times, the Pekingese was deemed sacred in China. Stealing a member of the breed resulted in a death sentence for the thief. *Right:* Tibet is the original home of the Lahsa Apso, which seems to hide behind its fall of fur. The ten-inch dog comes in all colors and sometimes lives to be 16 years old.

Preceding page: The dignified and majestic Afghan hound is the unofficial national dog of Afghanistan. It is said to be the dog breed that Noah chose to take on his ark. A fast runner, it can reach speeds of up to 28 miles per hour. *Above:* A lean dog, the borzois (also known as Russian wolfhound) is prone to running off spontaneously if it is tempted by the scent of game.

The whippet is actually a terrier modified with greyhound blood, capable of jack-rabbit starts clocked at 37 miles per hour. *Below:* The fastest dog on Earth, the greyhound ("great hound") was known in Egypt thousands of years before the Pharaohs. Second in speed only to the cheetah, it can move at 45 miles per hour. *Opposite:* Only dogs with a finely tuned sense of smell and a keen hunting instinct are used in fox hunts.

The U.S. Disaster Team Canine Search and Rescue Unit, founded in 1985, was established to locate victims of disasters such as hurricanes, earthquakes, floods, and mud slides. These dogs pick up human scents in the air and alert their handlers to the location of a victim. They can even distinguish between victims who are still alive and those who have died, enabling rescue crews to focus their efforts on areas where lives can be saved.

While the foxhound, which comes in many colors, appears to be docile and calm, it can expend a great deal of energy while on the trail of a fox. *Below:* When hounds come together during trials or a hunt, they truly become a "pack" of dogs. Most breeds have the pack instinct and will do anything necessary to stay in favor of the leader.

Grouse hunting is a popular sport for dogs and their human companions. *Below:* The stance of the pointer indicates the presence and position of game. The dog maintains an erect overall posture while bent forward with a front paw raised.

Other units are always on standby because the dogs can only work a few days at a time.

Dogs have also been recruited for war, up through the twentieth century. They were trained to carry tear gas and explosives, and to actually attack the opposition. The Doberman, German shepherd, and Rottweiler, were often used because of their dark coloring. Today, dogs are kept mainly as house pets, some as fine family watchdogs.

Assuming a statuesque and motionless stance, pointers assist the hunter by pointing when they detect the presence of unsuspecting game. *Opposite:* Although it is not officially recognized by the American Kennel Club, the Hungarian Vizsla is making a name for itself among American hunters.

A home watchdog's job is to bark...and bark...and bark. Its function is to announce and intimidate intruders. There are many canines who fit the watchdog bill, but some are more suited to the job than others. A dog with an assertive personality, a sense of territory, and protective instincts is perfect for the job.

Toy breeds, such as the diminutive Yorkshire terrier and the toy poodle, make good watchdogs. So do Doberman pinschers, German shepherds, boxers and corgis. The big voices of the mastiff, bull mastiff, Great Dane and Rottweiler are very effective in intimidating strangers. The bulldog, a nonsporting breed, is a good choice, too. Mixed-breed (mongrel) dogs can also make super watchdogs, as well as good companions.

Because of the gentle side of its disposition, the dog has been able to fill other niches for man. Seeing eye and hearing ear dogs are commonplace in today's society, working as helpers and companions for handicapped people.

Dogs have become regular visitors at nursing homes, helping to bring noncommunicative people out of their shells by allowing these patients to stroke them. This kind of interaction has also been shown to reduce high blood pressure and to have a soothing effect on psychotherapy patients.

The spaniels, according to AKC lists, include the English springer spaniel (pictured) as well as the American water spaniel, Clumber spaniel, cocker spaniel, English cocker spaniel, field spaniel, Irish water spaniel, Sussex spaniel and Welsh springer spaniel. *Left:* **The King Charles spaniel, or English toy spaniel, is primarily a companion dog.**

Cocker spaniels are even-tempered, respectful of their owners, and make good apartment pets. *Right:* Dogs with lop ears, like this English springer spaniel, are at risk for ear infections and parasites. Their ears should be checked daily for potential problems. *Following pages, left:* People who own Irish water spaniels insist that they have a sense of humor. They also have excellent hunting skills, particularly in retrieving downed fowl from water. *Right:* Dogs can sleep up to 16 hours a day if given the chance. Rest is one of the essentials for a happy dog, along with food, water, exercise, and grooming.

Some dogs even work for other dogs, taste-testing food at major dog food companies. They often work as "actors" for these and other companies in TV commercials. Many times, the dog has been elevated to star status in entertainment by performing tricks in television and film. Lassie, Tramp, Rin Tin Tin, and Benji have all become a unique part of American culture.

It's not all glamour and fan mail for these pooches, though. One such acting dog was known to respond to 200 voice commands and 70 hand gestures. The average dog knows about 10 or 15 basic commands.

With repetition, reward, and an atmosphere of fun and community, most dogs can master simple commands such as "sit," "stay," "come," "heel," "down," "out," "fetch," "no," "good dog," "bad dog", and a few other essentials. Some people have even taught their seemingly average dogs to do human tasks and activities such as parachuting, surfing, and unlocking car doors. Perceptive pooches have picked up on words and conversations without their owner's intention, so it is important to be aware of what is being said and how.

It's hard to resist taking one of these Beagle puppies home, but it's a good idea to keep puppies with their mothers until they are at least six weeks old. During that time, they will learn essential social skills which will help them adapt to family life. *Opposite:* In the top-ten list of registrations for many years, beagles are remarkable hunting dogs, as well as great companions.

Preceding page: **Famous as a good-natured family dog, the droopy-eyed basset hound's short legs and crooked knees allow it to hold its nose close to the ground. These dogs have an excellent sense of smell, making them good hunters.**
Above: **Independent, with a baritone voice, the bloodhound hails from Belgium and is also an enthusiastic hunter.**

A descendent of the bloodhound, the Weimaraner was at one time a big-game dog used in hunting wolves, wild cats, deer, bear, and other prey. *Below:* A large dog, reaching up to 27 inches at the shoulders, the Weimaraner (pronounced Vy-mah-rah-ner) is not happy when relegated to the kennel.

Dogs also pick up on the family's daily routine, knowing when to wake, when someone usually leaves the house, when the daily vitamin pill is taken, that bedtime is after the evening news theme, and that the leader of the pack pulls into the driveway soon after the school bus drops off the neighborhood kids.

From the day that a puppy becomes part of the household, it is the owner's responsibility to see that it gets adequate food and water, a comfortable place to sleep, exercise, play, and grooming. Veterinary care, in the form of inoculations and annual check-ups, is also a must.

Dogs have been the source of pleasure and pride for many people. It is clear that dog owners are also dog lovers, and anyone who has ever made friends with a dog knows why – they offer protection, companionship, and unconditional love. They give us something to hug and something to care for. And all they desire in return is to be a part of our lives.

Top to bottom: As its name implies, the Labrador retriever is a hunting dog, with an excellent sense of smell. On the list of top five breeds in both America and England, it is a duck dog par excellence and dominates in American retriever trials. "Labs" are born with some retrieving instincts, but they must be taught, with the use of sticks and other objects, the correct way to respond to retrieving commands. *Opposite:* Year-round pets that enjoy family activities, Labrador retrievers are also useful as guides for the blind.

A water dog, the Labrador retriever's double coat is actually water-resistant. The ideal Lab is slightly longer than it is tall, with a muscular build. *Right:* Although the word "golden" is part of the name of the Golden retriever, the breed actually comes in gold, cream, and wheat. *This page:* Known as the "happy breed," the Golden retriever is loyal, gentle, outgoing, and loves everyone. *Left:* Adult Golden retrievers weigh up to 75 pounds and need lots of exercise. *Opposite:* Dogs can be trained to do just about anything: come when called, roll over, get the newspaper or mail, hunt, care for people, and even jump over fences.

The English setter gets its name from its style of hunting—it tends to creep towards prey, sinking slowly between the shoulder blades as it points. *Below:* Boasting a silky chestnut or mahogany coat, the Irish setter is thought to be the only setter which is actually a spaniel.

Once trained to hunt, Irish setters will adapt to almost any terrain and climate. Their hunting skills remain with them throughout life.

Children and puppies seem to be soulmates. But it's wise not to leave them together unattended as each has tendencies to unintentionally hurt the other. *Opposite:* A true companion dog with a sense of adventure will go just about anywhere with its master—even windsurfing.

Index of Photography

TIB indicates The Image Bank.